Today's Superst★rs

Entertainment

Kelly Clarkson

by Doris Fisher

GARETH**STEVENS**

GS
P U B L I S H I N G
A Member of the WRC Media Family of Companies

Please visit our web site at: www.garethstevens.com
For a free color catalog describing Gareth Stevens Publishing's
list of high-quality books and multimedia programs, call
1-800-542-2595 (USA) or 1-800-387-3178 (Canada).
Gareth Stevens Publishing's fax: (414) 332-3567.

Library of Congress Cataloging-in-Publication Data

Fisher, Doris.
    Kelly Clarkson / by Doris Fisher.
       p. cm. — (Today's superstars. Entertainment)
    Includes bibliographical references and index.
    ISBN-13: 978-0-8368-7649-9 (lib. bdg.)
    1. Clarkson, Kelly, 1982- —Juvenile literature. 2. Singers—United States—
Biography—Juvenile literature. [1. Clarkson, Kelly, 1982- 2. Singers.] I. Title.
ML3930.C523F57   2007
782.42164092—dc22
[B]   2006030682

This edition first published in 2007 by
Gareth Stevens Publishing
A Member of the WRC Media Family of Companies
330 West Olive Street, Suite 100
Milwaukee, WI 53212 USA

Editor: Gini Holland
Art direction and design: Tammy West
Picture research: Sabrina Crewe

Photo credits: cover, p. 16 © Chris Pizzello/Reuters/Corbis; p. 5 © Lucy Nicholson/
Reuters/Corbis; pp. 7, 19 Getty Images; p. 9 © Chris Farina/Corbis; p. 11 © Tom Fox/
Dallas Morning News/Corbis; pp. 12, 15 Associated Press; p. 18 © Derick A. Thomas/
Dat's Jazz/Corbis; p. 20 © Fred Prouser/Reuters/Corbis; p. 25 Lester Cohen/
WireImage.com; p. 26 © 20th Century Fox/courtesy Everett Collection; p. 27
Everett Collection; p. 28 © Mike Blake/Reuters/Corbis

Printed in the United States of America

1 2 3 4 5 6 7 8 9 10 10 09 08 07 06

Contents

Chapter 1

A Big Dream

On a dim stage, a singer stood before the audience. She held a microphone. When the lights came up, the crowd saw her floor-length red gown. She had perfect makeup and long blond hair. The twenty-three-year-old was ready to sing. On this special night, she looked like a superstar.

The date was February 8, 2006. The event was the forty-eighth annual Grammy Awards in Los Angeles. Many of the big names in popular music were there. Sir Paul McCartney of the Beatles was in the hall. Mariah Carey, Alicia Keyes, and Stevie Wonder were there. Madonna, Bruce Springsteen, and Christina Aguilera were also at the show. All these stars gave out awards, performed, or sat in the audience.

Charming the Crowd

First, the audience screamed. Then, when the orchestra started to play, the crowd quieted down. The star started to sing. Her rich voice filled the hall as she sang her 2004 hit, "Because of You."

Fans all over the world knew her name. They also recognized her face. They had been to her concerts. They had seen her movie. She was the first winner of the television show, *American Idol: The Search for a Superstar.* She was Kelly Clarkson,

Kelly Clarkson performs "Because of You" at the nationally televised *48th Grammy Awards* in 2006.

charming the crowd and TV viewers across the country.

On the Grammy stage, Kelly Clarkson performed in front of the musicians she had admired for years. She also won two Grammy awards that night. One was for Best Female Pop Vocal Performance for her single, "Since U Been Gone." The second one was for Best Pop Vocal Album for *Breakaway*.

Years before this magical night, Kelly had talked about winning a Grammy. She'd dreamed about performing at the *Grammy Awards Show*. At the age of nineteen, Kelly said, "I have dreamed since I've been a little girl that I wanted to be on the *Grammys*. Everybody is at the awards show. And to be able to perform for people in the industry — people that you've looked up to since you were little — oh, that's the highest!"

She had worked hard. She had believed in her goals. Finally, in 2006, her Grammy dream came true!

Fact File

Kelly's favorite singer is Reba McIntire. Her favorite food is frozen Ding Dongs. She likes to say, "Cool beans!" when she thinks something is great, and her nickname is Kellbell.

The Grammy Awards

The Grammy Awards are held every year. The awards are presented by the music industry in America for outstanding music recordings. Professional musicians vote to name the winners. Grammys are not based on the number of records sold, but on how good the music is. Thirty different kinds of music can get a Grammy. These include pop and rap.

Winners receive a trophy shaped like a small gramophone. A gramophone is an antique record player. Emile Berliner invented it in 1887. The records were made of glass at first, and later they were made of plastic. The gramophone would spin the record. The "arm" of the gramophone held a needle that "read" the vibrations recorded in the grooves of the record. The needle then sent the information to the gramophone speaker. Then the listener heard the music.

The Grammys were first named The Gramophone Awards. They were first presented in 1959.

Kelly Clarkson poses with her Best Pop Vocal Album and Best Female Pop Vocal Performance awards at the 48th Grammy Awards on February 8, 2006.

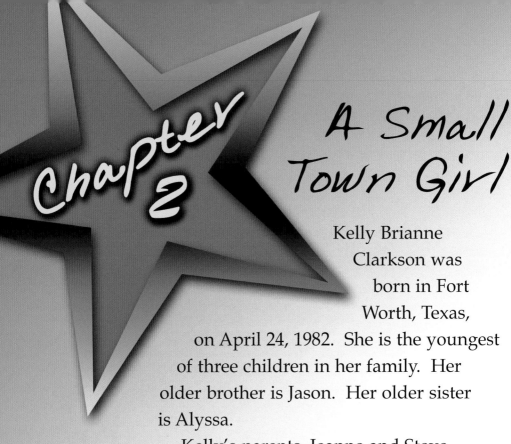

Chapter 2

A Small Town Girl

Kelly Brianne Clarkson was born in Fort Worth, Texas, on April 24, 1982. She is the youngest of three children in her family. Her older brother is Jason. Her older sister is Alyssa.

Kelly's parents, Jeanne and Steve Clarkson, divorced when she was six years old. The divorce split up the three children. Jason went to live with his father. Alyssa moved in with an aunt, and Kelly stayed with her mother. Kelly's father and brother later moved to California.

Jeanne Clarkson worked one job after another. She tried hard to support herself and Kelly. They moved many times before Kelly was in the fifth grade. It was hard to make friends each time they moved. Kelly

Kelly Clarkson gives her mother a hug as they arrive at the BMG Grammy After Party.

did not understand why they moved so often. "There were always worries financially," remembers Kelly. They finally settled down after moving to Burleson, Texas. Located south of Fort Worth, the population was about 14,000. Eventually, Jeanne married Jimmy Taylor, Kelly's stepfather.

Fact File

In her 2004 hit, "Because of You," Kelly wrote lyrics to express a child's confusion after a divorce. "Because of you," she wrote, "I find it hard to trust not only me, but everyone around me. Because of you, I am afraid."

As a child, Kelly loved to perform in the living room. She sang and acted in her own shows based on *Beauty and the Beast* and *The Little Mermaid*. She thought it was family fun, but she did not take singing or acting seriously.

Finding her Voice

When Kelly was in middle school, Mrs. Cynthia Glenn, the choir teacher, heard her singing in the hall. Mrs. Glenn asked her to join the school choir. "I actually didn't know I could sing until I was about thirteen," recalls Kelly. Many singers start voice training in grade school. In middle school, Kelly made up for lost time with hard work.

According to Mrs. Glenn, Kelly "would be working or practicing in her seat when everyone else was talking and laughing. She did not like to waste her time."

When the choir practiced scales, it was clear Kelly had an amazing voice. She could sing high and low notes other voices could not reach. Because of her

Fact File

Kelly thought she wanted to be a marine biologist. At the movies, the killer shark in *Jaws* really scared her. "I left that dream right there!" she says.

Hollywood, CA Burleson, TX

special voice, she could sing songs many other singers couldn't handle.

Kelly practiced making her own recordings at home. She didn't just use a tape recorder. She had a karaoke machine in her closet. Karaoke singing is often done in front of an audience. It's fun for the singer and the crowd. Karaoke machines were first used in Japan in the 1970s. The word *karaoke* means "empty orchestra" in Japanese. But Kelly's closet was more than an "empty orchestra." She hung a sign on the door that read, "Kelly's Recording Studio."

On a live broadcast of the *American Idol* show, Kelly talks with some of her best friends in the Burleson High gymnasium.

Fact File

Kelly sang her first solo in seventh grade. It was "Vision of Love" by Mariah Carey. "I never get nervous on stage," says Kelly.

Fact File

Kelly also liked sports in high school. She played soccer, volleyball, and basketball.

Practice and training gave her the skills she needed. Kelly never had private singing lessons. She is grateful to her choir teacher, Mrs. Glenn. "I have to give props to Cindy Glenn," she says, "for classically training me." Kelly sang all through high school. She also sang at church and at home. She joined the Texas All-State Choir. In high school, she sang in the musicals *Seven Brides for Seven Brothers* and *Brigadoon*. By the time Kelly graduated from high school, in 2000, she knew she wanted a career in music.

High Hopes in California

Chapter 3

After high school, Kelly Clarkson focused on her music career. She stayed in Burleson while most of her friends went to college. Kelly worked in a movie theater, in a pharmacy, and as a waitress. These jobs paid the bills, but they were not a way to get ahead in music.

Whenever she had spare time, she wrote songs. She recorded a demo CD and sent copies to record companies. She hoped to find someone interested in her singing. In spite of all her hard work, Kelly did not land a record deal. Early in 2002, she and a friend moved to Los Angeles, California. Perhaps living closer to record companies would make it easier to start her career.

Making the Rounds

Kelly went to many musical auditions in Los Angeles. Thinner and prettier girls seemed to get all the jobs.

Just a few record labels in LA expressed interest in Kelly. They wanted her to sing bubble-gum music and country music. These styles fit her perky, girl-next-door look. But Kelly knew she had more to offer. She had a natural gift for singing different kinds of music. She wanted to sing rock, soul, blues, and hip-hop, too. She didn't want to be known for only one type of singing. Record companies said Kelly could not succeed if she sang the kinds of music that were usually sung by African Americans. Kelly recalls that she "had so many doors closed because they said, 'It's not going to work. You're a little white girl.'"

Kelly didn't know what else to do. She still wanted to find someone who would help her get started in a singing career. She did land a few small parts on TV. Once, she was an

Fact File

Kelly tried to lose weight in LA. Then she realized she didn't want to change her looks. "I'm very curvy and I love it," she says. "I think girls get way too caught up in how they should look. I don't think you should have to be anybody but yourself, take it or leave it."

Kelly Clarkson promotes her new album *Breakaway* by performing on NBC's *Today Show* in New York City on May 23, 2005.

extra in an episode of *Sabrina, the Teenage Witch*. She never spoke or sang a single word in the show!

After Kelly met big-name songwriter Gerry Goffin, she thought her chances for a record contract would get better. He asked Kelly to make demos of some of his songs. Sadly, when Goffin became ill, their work together ended. Kelly's hopes of making records in California faded away.

Fact File

Kelly had little money in Los Angeles. She worked at many different jobs. "I always had three or four at a time," she says. "I was at rock bottom, so where could I go from there but up?"

Aretha Franklin

Kelly enjoyed singing hits recorded by Aretha Franklin. Known as the Queen of Soul, Aretha Franklin also sang blues, R & B, pop, and gospel music. In the late 1960s and 1970s, she was one of the most famous African American women in music. By most people's standards, she still rules as the Queen of Soul.

Aretha Franklin performs her classic hit "Respect" at the *10th Annual Soul Train Lady of Soul Awards* in 2005.

From Auditions to Idol

As Kelly's hopes began to fade, her daily life became worse. Her apartment burned down in 2002. She was twenty years old. She had little money and no place to live. She felt she needed to return to Texas. She drove home twenty-four hours without stopping!

Back in Burleson, Kelly worked hard. She sold the energy drink Red Bull and waited on tables in a comedy club. She still wanted a singing career. "No matter how many doors slam in your face, there's one that's waiting for just you," says Kelly.

Kelly's friend, Jessica Huggins, learned talent auditions were going to take place in Dallas. Jessica filled out the paperwork for Kelly. All Kelly had to do was sign the forms. Then she had to show up in Dallas

the next day. Kelly did not know the reason for the auditions.

Kelly stayed up all night. She was afraid the alarm would not wake her. Jeanne, Kelly's mother, remembers that many mornings, "The alarm clock would be blasting right beside her head, and she (wouldn't) hear a thing."

Early the next day, Kelly and Jessica drove to Dallas. It was about 40 miles (64 kilometers) from Burleson. Kelly was the first in line. She had to sing early because they had to drive back to Burleson in time for Kelly's jobs.

Kelly found out she was auditioning for a new TV show. It was called *American Idol: The Search for a Superstar*. The singers had to be between the ages of sixteen and twenty-four. Only eleven people at the Dallas tryouts made it to the second round. Kelly was one of them! The show flew her to California — for free — for more auditions.

Fact File

For one of her auditions, Kelly sang "At Last," a hit made by the legendary rhythm and blues singer Etta James. In 1961, "At Last" rose to the number two spot on the R & B chart for Etta James .

Weeks of Singing

The *American Idol* judges were Paula Abdul, Randy Jackson, and Simon Cowell. They listened to one hundred twenty singers in California. On the first day, they narrowed the group of singers down to sixty-five. Then, they cut the group to forty-five on the second day. After three days, the top thirty singers remained. Kelly made it to this select group.

Each finalist sang every week for thirteen television shows. A live audience listened to them. The judges commented on each song. Viewers voted for their favorite singer after each show.

Idol judges Randy Jackson, Paula Abdul, and Simon Cowell pose at the final show of *American Idol* in 2005.

Fact File

One thousand singers auditioned in Dallas. A total of ten thousand singers in the United States tried out for the first *American Idol*.

When Kelly won the competition of *American Idol*, she sang "A Moment Like This" to end the show in 2002. The losing singers give her support — and a little envy!

The first round of *American Idol* pitted the top thirty singers against each other for three weeks. Now they had to please the TV audience as well as the judges. Kelly belted out Aretha Franklin's smash hit, "Respect," on her first night. Her powerful voice thrilled the audience. Even hard-to-please judge Simon Cowell liked Kelly. The next night on *American Idol*, the judges told Kelly she had made it into the Top Ten.

Kelly's fans loved her big, rich voice. Kelly was also friendly. She wore no makeup in many of the everyday TV shots. For a stylish look, Kelly chose dressy outfits to wear when she sang on the show.

The final show was September 3, 2002. Only Kelly and Justin Guarini were left to sing. They each sang three solos. *American Idol* chose two of the songs they had to sing. They could choose their own third song.

Kelly chose "Respect," the same tune she had sung on *American Idol* earlier. More than eighteen million viewers watched. Fans cheered. The judges rocked along with the crowd. Kelly was hot!

The judges announced the winner on the next night's show, September 4, 2002. The audience screamed. Kelly recalls, "I couldn't hear them say I won. I actually found out when Justin hugged me and said, 'Congratulations!'" Kelly had won with fifty-eight percent of the votes.

For her last *American Idol* performance, Kelly sang "A Moment Like This." The song fit this special night. Tears streamed down her face. "Oh, I can't believe it's happening to me," she sang. "Some people wait a lifetime for a moment like this." Kelly Clarkson's wait was over. Her once-in-a-lifetime moment had arrived!

Fact File

Kelly sang so much during *American Idol* that her throat became raw and sore. Throat lozenges didn't help, but drinking olive oil did! Over and over, she forced herself to drink it to keep her voice in shape.

21

Chapter 5

American Idol in Action

Kelly won a one million dollar recording contract with RCA as the first "American Idol."

The next week, she was at the Lincoln Memorial in Washington, D. C. It was the first anniversary of the September 11, 2001, attack on the United States. Kelly sang the national anthem. This special event honored the men and women who had lost their lives due to the attack.

Two weeks after *American Idol*, Kelly released her first single record. "A Moment Like This" and "Before Your Love" were on a double A-side single. The record started on the singles chart at number fifty-two. It became number one in just one week. The *Billboard* Hot 100 Singles Chart had never seen a new record shoot to the top of its list so fast.

Kelly also toured the country with the nine other *American Idol* finalists. They sang in thirty U.S. cities.

A Singing Sensation

Thankful, Kelly's first album, was released in 2003. The album had many different kinds of music. Said Kelly, "There's soul. I have some rock on there. I have some big bluesy numbers and I have two ballads . . . and some faster, hip-hoppy stuff." It sold one million copies in one month, making it a "platinum" record. Eventually, it sold two million copies, which made it "double platinum."

Three songs from her album *Thankful*, "Miss Independent," "Low," and "The Trouble With Love," made the *Billboard* Top 10. "Miss Independent" was number one for five weeks.

Not Always a Winner

In June 2003, when Kelly was twenty-one, she starred in a movie with *American Idol* runner-up Justin Guarini. *From Justin*

Fact File

The A-side of a record features a song that may become a hit. The B-side of a record has a song that is considered not as important as the A-side song. A double A-side single record has songs on both sides that might become popular hits.

to Kelly was a musical with ten songs.
The movie's theme was spring break.
It showed lots of fun and beach scenes.
Kelly and Justin learned that making a
movie is different from singing on stage.
Movie scenes are shot over and over until
they are exactly right. The movie was
made in the winter. The pool and beach
water was very cold. They had to pretend
it was summer! They worked hard, but
the movie was not a success. Critics
thought it was one of the worst movies
of the year.

Platinum Singing Star
During December 2003, Kelly competed
for the title of World Idol in London,
England. The winner was Kurt Nilsen
from Norway. Kelly placed second — in
the world!

Breakaway was Kelly's second album,
released in 2004. Kelly was twenty-
two years old. *Breakaway* sold
five million copies, making
it "five times" platinum.
Her star really shined.

Fact File

A single record or an album
is called a gold record or album
when it has sold one-half million copies.
When a single album or record has sold
one million copies, it is called platinum.

In 2003, Kelly Clarkson proudly holds her framed platinium album award for *Thankful*.

Billboard

Billboard is a weekly magazine about music. It ranks popular songs and albums. It is highly respected in the music industry, so it is read by fans and musicians, alike. The *Billboard* Hot 100 rates the top one hundred singles of all kinds of music. The *Billboard* 200 is a chart for top album sales.

Kelly Clarkson and
Justin Guarini walk
together in a scene
from their 2003
movie, *From Justin
To Kelly*.

The songs from *Breakaway* in the *Billboard* Top 10 were, "Since U Been Gone," "Behind These Hazel Eyes," and "Because of You." The song "Since U Been Gone" was number one for eight weeks.

Kelly sang "Breakaway" and "Since U Been Gone" on *Saturday Night Live* in 2005. She was also a guest on *The Oprah Winfrey Show* and *The View*. The 2005 *American Music Awards* named her Artist of the Year and Favorite Adult Contemporary Artist.

Kelly received more honors. She won The People's Choice award for Favorite Female Performer in January 2006. She

Reality TV Contests

Reality TV shows have ordinary people on them, not paid actors. The people don't have written lines to say on the show. They hope to win a prize by being the last person left on the show. Sometimes, viewers vote to say who stays on the show each week.

Reality shows usually test how the people get along with each other. Shows can be about living on an island, being the best dancer, or working for a business giant like Donald Trump or Martha Stewart. The best prize from shows like the *American Idol* is usually a great new career for the winner.

Kelly Clarkson sings at a concert on the ABC television show *Good Morning America* in 2003.

27

won her two Grammys in February. Then, in April, she won The 2006 Kids' Choice award for Favorite Female Performer.

Kelly's Texas roots remain deep. She lives in California, but she also has a ranch near Fort Worth. "I'm always going to live in Texas," says Kelly. "Just 'cause Texas is so awesome — and everything else isn't."

Kelly Clarkson greets her fans at the 2006 MTV Video Music Awards.

As for her future, Kelly says, "Dudes, just let me sing. It doesn't matter to people how you got into the business. It matters to them how you stay." Her hard work has paid off. She is truly a shining superstar.

Time Line

1982	Kelly Brianne Clarkson is born in Fort Worth, Texas, on April 24.
2002	Wins the reality TV show *American Idol: The Search for a Superstar* September 4. Sings the national anthem at the Lincoln Memorial in Washington, D.C., on the first anniversary of the September 11, 2001 terrorist attack on the United States. "A Moment Like This," a hit single, sells 236,000 copies the first week it is released.
2003	Releases her first album, *Thankful*. Stars in the movie *From Justin to Kelly* with Justin Guarini, *American Idol* runner-up. Places second in the *World Idol* TV show held in London, England.
2004	Releases her second album, *Breakaway*.
2005	Appears on the TV shows *Saturday Night Live, The Oprah Winfrey Show*, and *The View*. Wins two American Music Awards: Artist of the Year and Favorite Adult Contemporary Artist.
2006	Wins The People's Choice Favorite Female Performer, Grammys for Best Female Pop Vocal Performance and Best Pop Vocal Album, and a 2006 Kids' Choice award.

Glossary

auditions — tryout performances to show one's ability or skill.

bubble-gum music — music made for ages ten to fifteen, with bouncy rhythms and cheerful tones.

contemporary — current or modern.

demo — short for demonstration; a recording made to show the ability of a musician or performer.

extra — a performer hired to play a minor part.

lozenges — medicated candies that dissolve in the mouth to soothe a sore throat.

lyrics — the words of a song.

marine biologist — a scientist who studies sea plants and animals.

R & B — short for rhythm and blues music, which has a strong beat and sings about sadness.

pop — a short term for popular music.

props — proper respect.

scales — in music, musical notes going up or down in order of pitch.

solo — a performance by only one singer or entertainer.

soul — African American gospel singing closely related to rhythm and blues music.

To Find Out More

Books

Kelly Clarkson. Young Profiles (series). Jill C. Wheeler (ABDO Publishing)

Working in Music and Dance. My Future Career (series). Margaret McAlpine (Gareth Stevens)

Videos

From Justin to Kelly. (Twentieth Century Fox) PG

Audio CDs

Thankful. RCA

Breakaway. RCA

Web Sites

Kelly Clarkson
www.kellyclarksonweb.com
Photos, news, song lyrics

American Idol
www.americanidol.com
News, photos, contestants

Publishers note to educators and parents: Our editors have carefully reviewed these Web sites to ensure that they are suitable for children. Many Web sites change frequently, however, and we cannot guarantee that a site's future contents will continue to meet our high standards of quality and educational value. Be advised that children should be closely supervised whenever they access the Internet.

Index

About the Author

Doris Fisher writes picture books, magazine articles, poetry, word puzzles, and mazes for children. She is a former kindergarten teacher. Doris lives in a suburb of Houston, Texas, with her husband and Comet, their pet Maltese. Their son and daughter are grown. She dedicates this book to Charles Trevino, a wonderful writer who encourages all of her writing ideas!